Dear Sister

from you to me®

This book is for your Sister's unique and amazing story.

It is for her to capture some of her life's key memories, experiences and feelings.

Ask her to complete it carefully and, if she wants to, add some photographs or images to personalise it more.

When it is finished and returned to you, this will be a record of her story . . . a story that you will treasure forever.

Dear

Here is my letter to you ...

Tell me about the time and place you were born . . .

What are your earliest memories?

Tell me about your childhood . . .

What do you think people thought about you as a child?

What do you remember about the place/s you lived when you were young?

What were your favourite childhood toys or games?

Tell me about your best childhood friend/s...

What do you remember about any holidays you had when you were young?

What did you enjoy about your school days?

What did you want to do when you grew up?

Tell me about the hobbies you had when you were young . . .

What family traditions do you continue to follow?

Being the **eldest, youngest** or a **middle** sibling can be **different**.

Describe what it is like for you . . .

If you could, what would you swap with me?

What **family values** have you learnt that you would like to pass on to others?

Tell me some of your favourite family stories . . .

Did you have an idol when you were young?
Tell me who and why . . .

Who was your first love and why?

What was the first piece of music you bought?

Tell me about your first job and some of the other work you have done . . .

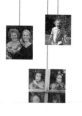

Describe some of your fondest memories of the times we have spent together . . .

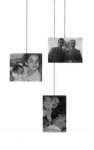

Describe the funniest things that have happened to us . . .

Tell me what you like about me . . .

What is the most annoying thing I have done?

Is there anything you would change about me?

What will you remember me for?

What would you still love us to do together?

What are the happiest or greatest memories
of your life?

Tell me about the things that make you happy or laugh...

What piece/s of music would you choose in your own favourite 'top 10'?

Tell me what would make up your favourite
meal ...

Describe your favourite way of spending a weekend ...

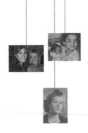

What would you include in your top 10 views in the world?

What have been some of your best holiday destinations?

If you could live anywhere …

where would you live and why?

What are a few of your favourite things?

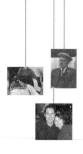

Describe your memory of some major world events that have happened in your lifetime . . .

If you could travel in time ...

where would you go to and why?

Describe the greatest change that you have seen in your lifetime so far . . .

If you were an **animal** . . . what **type** of animal would you be, and why?

If you won the Lottery . . . what would you do with the money?

Tell me about the goals and aspirations you have had for your life . . .

What do you still want to achieve in your life?

Is there anything you'd like to change about yourself?

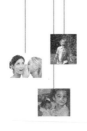

Tell me about the dreams you have for your life . . .

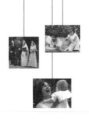

What can I do to help you achieve what you want?

What have you found most difficult in your life?

What is your **biggest regret** in your life?

Can you do anything about it **now**?

Is there anything you would like to say **sorry** for?

With hindsight what would you do **differently**?

If you were granted three wishes . . .

what would they be and why?

Tell me something you think I won't know about you . . .

What would you like your epitaph to say?

What is the best piece of advice you have
ever been given?

Given your experiences, what advice would you like to offer me?

And now your chance to write anything else
you want to say to me . . .

These extra pages are for us to write any **questions, memories** or **answers** that may not have been covered elsewhere in the book . . .

And finally for the record . . .

what is your full name ?

what is your date of birth ? .

what colour are your eyes ?

how tall are you ?

what blood group are you ?

what was the date when you completed this story for me ?

And a few words to thank you for completing this Journal of a Lifetime ...

If you liked the concept of this book, please tell your family and friends and look out for others in the current *from you to me* range.

Journals of a Lifetime
Dear Mum
Dear Dad
Dear Grandma
Dear Grandad
Dear Daughter
Dear Son
Dear Brother
Dear Friend

Home Gift Journals
Cooking up Memories
Digging up Memories

You can also use this code by downloading a free QR code reader app to your smart phone.

Sport Gift Journals
Kicking off Memories
Try to Remember

Personal Development Journals
Dear Future Me

Leaving Gift Journals
These were the Days
Primary School Journals

Parent & Baby
Mum to Mum ... pass it on
Bump to first Birthday ... pregnancy & first year journal
Our Story ... for my Daughter
Our Story ... for my Son

Christmas Memories
Christmas Past, Christmas Present

Personalised
You can personalise your own Journal of a Lifetime online at www.fromyoutome.com

All titles are available at gift and book shops or online at www.fromyoutome.com

Dear *Sister*

from you to me®

First published in the UK by *from you to me*, April 2008
Copyright, *from you to me* limited 2007/8
Hackless House, Murhill, Bath, BA2 7FH
www.fromyoutome.com
E-mail: hello@fromyoutome.com

ISBN 978-1-907048-04-3

Cover design by so design consultants www.so-design.co.uk

This book is printed on woodfree paper produced from a sustainable
source and Elemental Chlorine Free paper sourced to FSC standards.
Printed in India by Replika Press on behalf of JFDI print services Ltd.

If you think other questions should be included in future editions,
please let us know. And please share some of the interesting answers
you receive with us at the from you to me website to let other people
read about these fascinating insights . . .